WHAT IS A MONARCHY?

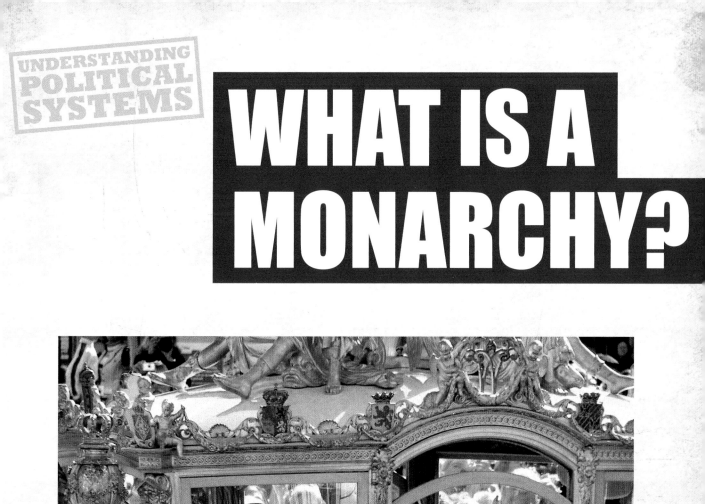

ROBYN HARDYMAN

 Gareth Stevens
Publishing

Please visit our website, www.garethstevens.com. For a free color catalog of all our high-quality books, call toll free 1-800-542-2595 or fax 1-877-542-2596.

Library of Congress Cataloging-in-Publication Data

Hardyman, Robyn.
What is a monarchy? / Robyn Hardyman.
    pages cm. — (Understanding political systems)
Includes index.
ISBN 978-1-4824-0315-2 (pbk.)
ISBN 978-1-4824-3302-9 (6-pack)
ISBN 978-1-4824-0314-5 (library binding)
1. Monarchy—Juvenile literature. I. Title.
JC375.H35 2014
321'.6—dc23
                        2013028415
First Edition

Published in 2014 by
Gareth Stevens Publishing
111 East 14th Street, Suite 349
New York, NY 10003

© 2014 Gareth Stevens Publishing

Produced by Calcium, www.calciumcreative.co.uk
Designed by Keith Williams and Paul Myerscough
Edited by Sarah Eason

Photo credits: Cover: Dreamstime: Waiheng (left), Shutterstock: Atlaspix (right). Inside: Dreamstime: 1000words 34, Braghetta 31, Emma98 42, Fainastock02 39, Featureflash 38, Instinia 5, Georgios Kollidas 15, 30, Martinapplegate 45, Phillipminnis 40, Prehor 4, Skilleddesigner 28; Shutterstock: Atlaspix 22, Andrey Burmakin 41, Devin Pavel 36, Featureflash 25, Goodluz 12, David P. Lewis 24, Nadezhda1906 43, Plrang 9, Igor Rogozhnikov 29, Andrey Starostin 23, Takepicsforfun 8; Wikimedia Commons: 7, 10, Jacques-Louis David, Google Art Project 17, U. Dettmar/Abr 32, Europicture.de 14, Hans Holbein the Younger, Google Art Project 44, Kollmeierf 33, Library of Congress 20, Manohar, Hermitage Museum 6, Holger Motzkau 21, Museen Nord/Bismarck Museum 19, Judge Oliver Seymour Phelps and Andrew T. Servin 16, Pivari 18, D. Gordon E. Robertson 13, Roel 1, 27, Royal Family of Bhutan 35, Cecil Stoughton, White House 37, Matthias Süßen 11, Allan Warren 21.

Printed in the United States of America

CPSIA compliance information: Batch # CW14GS: For further information contact Gareth Stevens, New York, New York at 1-800-542-2595.

Contents

CHAPTER ONE

What Is a Monarchy?

When we look back at history, we often think of a succession of rulers. They may have been pharaohs in Egypt, tsars in Russia, or kings and queens in Europe. All these rulers were monarchs. They held the highest office, or position, in their state. Monarchy is any system of government in which a monarch holds this office.

HEREDITARY MONARCHY

The monarch is also called the sovereign, or supreme ruler. For most of history, monarchs have inherited their role from a parent, or another close relative. They are not elected. The monarchy of a country has sometimes remained in the same royal family for hundreds of years. This is hereditary monarchy. When the monarch dies, the crown has traditionally passed to his or her oldest son, but today it may pass to a son or a daughter. If the monarch has no children, his or her nearest relative succeeds. In a republic, such as the United States, the head of state is a politician elected by the people.

This gold mask was made for the ancient Egyptian pharaoh, Tutankhamun, who died in 1323 BC. The pharaohs were the monarchs of ancient Egypt.

THE VALUE OF MONARCHY

One hundred years ago, most states around the world were monarchies. However, in the last century, most of the monarchies worldwide have disappeared. The advantages and disadvantages of having a nonelected head of state are still a source of argument.

"The monarchy is a political referee, not a political player, and there is a lot of sense in choosing the referee by a different principle from the players. It lessens the danger that the referee might try to start playing."

What do you think of this quote from historian, Conrad Russell, about the value of monarchy? What are the differences between a referee and a player?

CONSTITUTIONAL MONARCHY

In the past, monarchs had more power than they do today. They ruled with absolute authority. In more recent history, monarchs have given up most of their powers to institutions of democratic government, laid down in the country's constitution. This is called constitutional monarchy.

In a modern constitutional monarchy, the monarch's role is often ceremonial. In Britain, the Queen attends formal events such as the State Opening of Parliament. They are full of history and pageantry.

The History of Monarchy

Monarchy has been the most long-lasting form of government in history. The idea of rule by one single, powerful, hereditary leader began with the earliest of civilizations, more than five thousand years ago. Through the centuries, some of the jobs that monarchs carry out have changed, or disappeared. The monarchies that remain today are surprisingly different from each other, which is a reflection of these monarchies' rich and varied histories.

RELIGION AND WAR

For much of history, monarchs claimed that their right to rule was given by God. In some cases, they even claimed to be divine themselves. This gave them absolute authority to rule. Even when they did not claim to be divine, monarchs used the religion of their country, and its institutions, to support their position. European monarchs worked closely with the Christian Church. Religious ceremonies, such as coronations, showed that a king's authority was backed by the Church. Monarchs have often united warring peoples into larger, stronger states. For much of history, they were warriors themselves, who led their armies into battle. Many also tried to increase their power by conquering other countries.

Akbar was the Mughal emperor of India in the fourteenth century. He was the son of the previous emperor, and his son inherited the throne after him.

MAKING COUNTRIES WEALTHY

Monarchs tried to make their countries stronger by imposing law and order, and by making the countries richer. They often spread a system of laws across their country, and gave more people access to it. Monarchs also spent money on improving their country's armed forces, agriculture, and industry. Of course, monarchs often worked to make themselves richer, too! Any system of government that puts power in the hands of just one person is risky. The ruler may be incompetent, or make decisions that are not in the best interests of their country.

▲ A new monarch was officially given his or her title at a coronation. This painting shows the coronation of an emperor named Charlemagne, in 800 AD. He was king of the Franks, and he created a great empire in Europe. He was crowned by the Pope.

UNDERSTANDING BETTER

REPUBLIC OR MONARCHY?

Republics have almost always come into existence after a monarchy has failed in a country. The failure of monarchy may have been due to a crisis in which the ruling family collapsed, or a revolution in which a monarch was overthrown by his or her people. Republics have no king or queen as their head of state, but instead appoint an elected leader to govern over the state as president. Republics have often been selected when monarchy is no longer an option. Why do you think this might be?

Monarchy in the Ancient World

Monarchies began with the earliest civilizations. These were in Mesopotamia (modern-day Iraq), and Egypt. From these areas, the concept of monarchy spread to various parts of the world, such as India, the Middle East, and parts of the Mediterranean.

DIVINE CONNECTIONS

Most monarchs were kings because, historically, men were believed to be more suitable than women as a head of state. A monarch was regarded as a particularly special person who had powers given to him by the gods. People believed that their monarch's link with the gods ensured that their country would be protected. If times of hardship occurred, people believed it was a sign of the gods' displeasure. In India, emperor Asoka (c.265–238 BC) decided to set a moral example to his people. He stopped his warlike ways and ended his conquest of other countries. Asoka also converted to the Buddhist religion. The emperor brought peace and prosperity to his country, forbidding all use of violence, and even allowed other religions to be practiced. Asoka's rule brought about a "golden age" in India.

The ancient Egyptians believed the pharaoh was actually a god in human form. Pharaohs ordered the building of statues, like these of Rameses II outside his temple, so they would be remembered forever.

UNDERSTANDING BETTER

A WEAKNESS OF MONARCHY?

Ancient Rome saw much change of rule during its thousand-year history. The empire was first ruled by kings, then it became a republic. As the empire grew through conquest of other countries, powerful Roman generals seized power and became emperors. Some ruled well, others did not. The third emperor, Caligula (AD 37–41) was one of Rome's weakest rulers. He demanded to be worshipped as a god, treated people cruelly, and was very extravagant. Caligula's behavior was too much for his opponents, and the emperor was assassinated. What does this show about the danger of giving absolute power to one person? Is there always a solution to the problem?

CHINESE MONARCHS

In China, too, emperors ruled with the gods' favor, known as "the mandate of heaven." A succession of powerful emperors ruled China for almost 3,500 years, from around 1500 BC to 1911. If one ruling family, or dynasty, died out or was overthrown, another simply took its place. A Chinese dynasty could rule for several hundred years.

Emperor Caligula was a ruthless ruler.

Medieval Europe

After the end of the Roman Empire in the fifth century, Europe divided into many small kingdoms. By this time, most countries within Europe had become Christian. The power of monarchs and of the Church was now closely linked, and this would continue to be the case for hundreds of years to come.

CONFLICT AND RELIGION

The early medieval period in Europe was a time of wars, as neighboring states fought for land. Their rulers were warriors, who were usually chosen from one family. However, these monarchs could often be overthrown. In order to cement their power holds, monarchs turned to the Church for support. The exchange was simple, the Church helped to keep the monarch in power, and taught people to obey and fight for him. In return, the monarch supported the Church and increased its wealth and power. As nations began to settle and grow stronger, so did their kings. These monarchs had great authority, but they governed in partnership with their nobles and the Church, and had to consult them on many matters.

At the coronation of King Richard I of England at Westminster Abbey, London, in 1189, the king was anointed with holy oil by the Archbishop of Canterbury.

WARS AND CONQUEST

Going to war was an important part of the role of a medieval monarch. King Richard I of England (1189–1199) spent only five months of his reign in England. For the rest of his rule, Richard was either overseas defending his lands in France, or fighting a crusade, on behalf of the Church, against Islam in the Holy Land. Sometimes wars brought glory and greater power. Sometimes wars brought disaster. War was very expensive, and monarchs had to find the money to pay for them. They did this by demanding taxes from their subjects. They raised the levels of these taxes, and also created more efficient systems for collecting them. Both these measures were unpopular with people, especially if the wars did not go well and the army was defeated.

UNDERSTANDING BETTER

GODLIKE POWER

A king's coronation was a highly religious ceremony, used to strengthen the message that the king ruled with God's blessing. This image is of a mosaic in a church in Palermo, Sicily, that was created by the successors of King Roger II of Sicily. The mosaic shows Roger II's coronation in 1095, and in it he is being crowned directly by Jesus Christ. What message do you think Roger's successors wanted to give about the right to rule, not only of Roger II, but also of all kings?

In this mosaic, King Roger II of Sicily is receiving his crown directly from Christ.

Monarchy in the Americas

In the Americas, there were two powerful examples of monarchy. The Aztec Empire lasted from the fourteenth to the sixteenth centuries in Mexico. The Inca Empire was established in western South America, in modern Peru, in the fifteenth and sixteenth centuries. Both civilizations had sacred, or holy, monarchs.

THE MIGHTY AZTECS

The Aztec Empire included many different peoples, across a large area. Once an area had been conquered, its local leader was generally allowed to continue ruling, as long as taxes were paid to the central government. The emperor was called the Huey Tlatoani. He was the ultimate power, appointed by the gods. He decided the level of taxes to be paid by each area, and he took his country to war. He was usually succeeded by a family member, but not necessarily his son.

The Inca city of Machu Picchu was built high up on a mountain ridge for the emperor Pachacuti, in about 1450, but it was abandoned when the Spanish invaders arrived about one hundred years later.

THE POWERFUL INCA EMPIRE

The great Inca Empire included about 10 million people. Its emperor was called the Sapa Inca, which means "sole ruler." His huge empire was divided into four quarters, and was well organized and very efficient. The Incas believed that the emperor was a god and a descendant of Inti, the Inca god of the sun. Whenever the emperor left his palace, his face was covered with a cloth—showing that he was too sacred to be seen by the people.

Pachacuti (1438–1472) was the ninth Sapa Inca and an oppressive monarch.

UNDERSTANDING BETTER

POWERFUL LEADERS

Both the Aztec and the Inca empires were overthrown by a relatively small number of Spanish invaders in the 1500s. Why do you think the Spanish managed to defeat the empires, when their monarchs were so powerful? Ironically, the power of the monarchs was part of the reason why the Spanish were able to defeat them. The Spanish simply caught the monarchs, and then ruled through them. The Aztec and Inca people always obeyed their ruler, without question. When the Spanish made demands of the people through their emperors, the people did exactly what they were told. By the time the people of both empires realized that they were losing their independence, it was too late to reverse the situation.

Early Modern Europe

In the late medieval period in western Europe, monarchies became more and more powerful. This was especially true of monarchies in Spain, France, and England. In these countries, with the support of the Church, monarchs greatly increased their wealth and power, and their control over their people.

ABSOLUTE RULE

Powerful states set up institutions to put the monarch's wishes into action and collect taxes from the people. The power of the Church declined, and the power of royal armies increased.

THE SUN KING

One of the most powerful, and extraordinary, of monarchs in western Europe was the French king, Louis XIV (1643–1715). Louis ruled with absolute power, and even called himself the Sun King. He was wise enough to appoint very able ministers. They put his policies into action, and gave good advice, but it was the king who made the decisions. Louis also developed a dazzling court at Versailles, outside Paris. This, and Louis' firm control, inspired other absolute rulers, in Russia, and elsewhere. Louis also made mistakes, however. He took his country into one expensive war after another, and demanded high taxes to pay for them. He ruled without consulting parliament and, eventually, 75 years after his death, the French people rose up against this style of monarchy.

This painting of Louis XIV of France, as a young man, shows him as the god Jupiter. This was intended to strengthen the idea of his royal power.

RULING WITH PARLIAMENT

In England, King Henry VIII (1509–1547), and his daughter Elizabeth I (1558–1603), also strengthened their country. However, they were not absolute monarchs. Henry and Elizabeth worked with parliament, and had to seek approval from it in order to create laws and raise taxes. This tradition of consulting with a parliament, rather than ruling with absolute power, probably saved England from a revolution later, when King Charles I and the English parliament came into conflict in the 1640s.

UNDERSTANDING BETTER

HEALING POWERS

Scrofula is an infection that causes painful swellings on the neck. In France and England, it was known as the King's Evil, because it was believed that a "royal touch" could cure it. People gathered before the king, who touched each patient on the neck and gave them a gold coin. What does this tell you about how people viewed their king? In the days before effective modern medicine, can you imagine how desperate people would have been for cures?

▲ *This portrait of Elizabeth I in her coronation robes was designed to impress. She is covered in jewels and is holding the symbols of royal authority, the orb and scepter.*

Constitutional Monarchy

The institution of monarchy remained almost unchallenged until around 1770. At this time, new political ideas and changes in society began to limit royal power. People began to question the divine right of kings and queens to rule, and started to believe that people should have a much greater say in how their country was governed.

DECLARATION OF RIGHTS

In England in the mid-1600s, parliament rebelled against King Charles I, who had ruled unwisely and failed to consult parliament closely enough during his reign. In the civil war that followed, the king was executed and, for 12 years, England was a republic. After the monarchy was restored in 1660, English kings had to respect the will of parliament. In 1689, a Declaration of Rights was issued that clearly defined the more limited powers of the monarch. This was the beginning of what is known as constitutional monarchy, where the power of the monarch is limited by parliament. Over the next 200 years, more royal powers were transferred to the elected government.

This picture shows the trial of King Charles I, in 1649. He was accused of acting for his own good, rather than for the good of his people.

REPUBLICAN RULE

In France, a violent revolution took place in 1789 against the absolute rule of King Louis XVI, who was then executed. In 1805, Napoleon Bonaparte made himself emperor of the French, but eventually he too was deposed. Britain's colonies in America rebelled against the rule of the British monarch. The colonies became independent of Britain in 1783, and renamed themselves the United States of America. This large republic was a major challenge to monarchy in Britain, and elsewhere.

The French Revolution overthrew the monarchy, but the new republic was soon replaced by an empire. Emperor Napoleon Bonaparte controlled France, and much of Europe, until he was defeated in 1815.

UNDERSTANDING BETTER

IS MONARCHY A RIGHT?

This is part of the speech made by King Charles I at his trial, in 1649, during the English Civil War. The trial found Charles I guilty, and sentenced him to death.

"I would know by what power I am called hither … I mean lawful; there are many unlawful authorities in the world … Remember, I am your King, your lawful King, and what sins you bring upon your heads, and the judgment of God upon this land … I have a trust committed to me by God, by old and lawful descent. I will not betray it, to answer a new, unlawful authority."

Charles I argued strongly for God's protection of his position as king. What is the "unlawful authority" he spoke of?

New Kingdoms

The 1800s saw a lot of upheaval and change in Europe. With these sweeping changes, the system of rule and control within countries also changed. France finally became a republic in 1870, but elsewhere constitutional monarchies were created. This was the time when monarchy was at its height.

GREAT RULERS, HUGE TERRITORIES

In Germany and Italy, the states of each country were united into single kingdoms. In Germany, the new ruler was named the kaiser. In 1861, in Italy, the parliament proclaimed Victor Emmanuel II the newly unified country's first king. In southeast Europe, the Habsburg family ruled over the large Austrian Empire. In Russia, the Romanov family ruled as tsars, or emperors, of a vast territory that included most of northern and central Asia. In Britain, Queen Victoria reigned not only at home but also worldwide. She also married her children and grandchildren to members of other royal families, in Russia, Greece, Italy, Spain, Denmark, Portugal, and Germany. This gave her even more influence.

Before he became king of the whole country of Italy, Victor Emmanuel II was king of the regions of Piedmont, Savoy, and Sardinia. He then ruled the whole country until he died in 1878.

EMPIRES ABROAD

While monarchs strengthened their positions at home, many also took over new territories abroad. Large parts of Africa and Asia were colonized by the nations of Europe. During these colonizations, the British often allowed existing local rulers to remain in place, unless they abused their power, or resisted British rule. Britain allowed monarchs to stay in position in its colonies because, with a monarch as its own head of state, the country wanted to support the rule of kings. France, in contrast, which was now a republic, imposed republics on its colonies.

This painting shows King Wilhelm I of Prussia being declared the kaiser, or emperor, of Germany.

UNDERSTANDING BETTER

UNIFYING GERMANY

It is not always kings who push for greater power for their country. In 1871, the large and powerful country of Germany was created not by a king, but by a politician named Otto Von Bismarck. Bismarck was Chancellor of Prussia, which was at the time the biggest and most powerful of the German states. Bismarck wanted to create a rival to the powerful Austrian Empire, to the south of Prussia, so he set about unifying the German states. He did so by taking them to war against their common enemy—France. With the aim of defeating France, the German states agreed to join together. King of Prussia, William I, was made kaiser of Germany.

The Fall of Monarchies

The twentieth century brought about the end of most of the world's monarchies. It saw sweeping revolution in some countries, and two world wars that created enormous social and political change. As a result of these huge changes, many monarchies did not survive. The ones that did were often very different from each other.

REVOLUTION

The Russian Revolution of 1917 resulted in the execution of Tsar Nicholas II, and all his family. The revolutionaries were protesting against the absolute rule of this tsar, and his predecessors, over many years. They renamed Russia the Soviet Union and the country was then governed by one party alone, the Communist Party. In 1911, another revolution, this time in China, brought down the emperor, ending 2,000 years of imperial rule. China became a republic, and is now a communist nation today.

This photograph of the Russian tsar, Nicholas II, was taken shortly after he abdicated, or stood down as tsar, in 1917. A year later, he and his whole family were executed by the revolutionaries.

WORLD WARS

After their defeat in World War I, in 1918, the Habsburgs lost their Austrian Empire. The Turkish Empire, farther east, also collapsed. After World War II (1939–1945), Italy became a republic, and the old monarchies of eastern Europe became part of the Soviet Union. In the 1940s and 1950s, most monarchies in the Arab world became republics, too. As late as 1973, the monarchy of Greece was also abolished, following a popular referendum, or vote, in which the Greek people decided to finally end their rule by kings and queens.

King Constantine II of Greece went into exile when the army seized power in his country in 1967. Although the army soon lost power, the people of Greece voted to end the monarchy and Greece became a republic.

UNDERSTANDING BETTER

FREEDOM THROUGH INDEPENDENCE?

Between 1945 and 1975, the former colonies of European nations gained their independence. India became independent of Britain, and established itself as a federal, democratic republic. Many African countries became republics, too. However, in many African states, powerful individuals soon seized power and ruled as dictators. Civil wars often followed in these countries. Some historians argue that, in some ways, life in the colonies was better before independence, because the colonies were well run and peaceful under colonial rule. With independence came rule by dictatorship in many countries. The people there had as little say in their government after independence as before it. What do you think?

CHAPTER TWO

Modern Monarchies

Although many monarchies came to an end during the twentieth century, there remain more than two dozen monarchies around the world today. They are different from each other, and the amount of power that the monarch holds varies from one country to another.

CONSTITUTIONAL MONARCHIES

Most modern monarchies are constitutional and democratic. The constitution limits royal power and, instead, gives it to the institutions of government. These institutions are the executive, which makes and implements policy, the legislature, which debates and makes laws, and the judiciary, which ensures that the law is enforced fairly and equally for all citizens. The role of the monarch in a constitutional, democratic monarchy is symbolic. Monarchs are head of state, but they make no political decisions.

Queen Elizabeth II has been the monarch of Great Britain and Northern Ireland since 1952. She inherited the title from her father, King George VI. She does not "rule," but she is Head of State. In 2012, she celebrated her Diamond Jubilee, or 60 years as Queen.

DO MONARCHS STILL HAVE A PLACE?

Although a constitutional monarch has no political role, he or she can still advise their government about its policies. Can you think how this might be useful? If a monarch has reigned for a long time, they will have gained great experience of crises, wars, and other problems. They can also remain "above" politics, and take a view that is in the interests of the whole country. Queen Elizabeth II, for example, has reigned through the careers of 12 British prime ministers. She meets with the prime minister every week, to discuss the most important issues facing Britain.

A HOLY MONARCH

The Pope is the absolute, elected monarch of Vatican City. Although Vatican City lies within the city of Rome, it is an independent state. The Pope is also head of the Catholic Church around the world.

Elected by the cardinals of the Catholic Church, the Pope has control over the executive, legislature, and judiciary of Vatican City. Vatican City is the only remaining absolute monarchy in all of Europe.

Vatican City is a walled territory inside the city of Rome. It has a population of less than 1,000, and is the smallest independent state in the world. Its monarch is the head of the Roman Catholic Church, the Pope.

United Kingdom

The United Kingdom consists of England, Scotland, Wales, and Northern Ireland. It has one of the oldest monarchies in the world. The Queen reigns, but she does not rule. Her role is symbolic. She is head of state, but she does not make political decisions, policies, or laws. These are done by the government. The British monarchy is the model for most of the world's other constitutional monarchies today.

AN IMPORTANT ROLE

For many people in Britain, the monarch is a powerful symbol and focus for the nation. Queen Elizabeth II has reigned for more than 60 years and is a highly respected and admired figure, both at home and abroad. Along with inspiring loyalty and patriotism, the Queen performs many ceremonial roles. These include hosting foreign heads of state, state visits abroad, and handing out awards for public service. The Queen promotes the work of many charities, and is also Supreme Governor of the Church of England.

People turn out in great numbers when the Queen comes to visit. This happens in countries all over the world, not just in the United Kingdom. These crowds are in Ottawa, Canada. In her long reign, Queen Elizabeth has made more than 60 state visits to other countries.

UNDERSTANDING BETTER

MONARCHY FOREVER?

The British royal family has occasionally faced severe press criticism. The way in which the royal family is financed, and the marital problems of its junior members, have led to complaints from many people within Britain. Some people would like Britain to become a republic, and have called for an end to the monarchy. Despite this, support for the British monarchy remains high, and most people in Britain think it should continue. Why do you think this is? Is it because of the country's long history of monarchy? Perhaps it is because the present monarch performs her role so well? Can this loyalty continue? What do you think?

The British monarchy is hereditary. Prince Charles, the Queen's eldest son, is the current heir to the throne.

THE COMMONWEALTH

The British monarch is also the head of state in some foreign countries that were formerly part of the British Empire. Today, these countries are all independent nations, but are also members of the Commonwealth. This is a nonpolitical organization that encourages democracy and economic cooperation among its 54 member countries. The Queen is head of the Commonwealth, and its members include Canada, Australia, and India, as well as many African countries.

Monarchy in Europe

There are several constitutional monarchies left in Europe today. Most of them have very long histories. These monarchies are all largely similar to Britain's. The king or queen holds a powerful place in the life of the nation, but has no political power.

MANY MONARCHS

Denmark has been a monarchy for more than one thousand years. The present queen, Margrethe II, has reigned since 1972. Until 1905, Norway shared a monarch with Sweden, but since independence it has had its own sovereign, as has Sweden.

The Netherlands has had a monarchy since 1815, and Belgium since 1830. In all these cases, the monarch's main tasks are to represent their countries abroad and to be a unifying figure at home. Their work for charity is also very important.

Queen Margrethe II of Denmark celebrated 40 years on the throne in 2012.

TO REPUBLIC AND BACK

Some countries have experienced the turbulence of overthrowing their monarchy and becoming a republic, only to return to a system of monarchy once more. One such country is Spain. The country has a history of monarchy that dates back many centuries, but became a republic in 1931. A military dictator, General Franco, then seized power and controlled Spain for many years. After Franco died in 1975, the monarchy was restored. Since then, King Juan Carlos I has reigned.

Queen Beatrix of the Netherlands reigned from 1980 to 2013. Now that her son, Willem-Alexander, is king, she is called Princess Beatrix.

UNDERSTANDING BETTER

IS ABDICATION RIGHT?

Queen Beatrix of the Netherlands abdicated in April 2013, aged 75, as her mother and grandmother did before her. Her eldest son, Willem-Alexander, became the first king to reign in the Netherlands since 1890. Opinions differ about whether an elderly monarch should step down and make way for his or her younger heir. Some people argue that monarchs are appointed for life, so should therefore continue to reign until they die. In Britain, monarchs serve the country until they die. Do you think this is right? If not, how long do you think an heir should have to wait to take on the role they were born to?

CHAPTER THREE

Powerful Monarchies

There remain a handful of more powerful monarchies in the world, where the ruler has real political authority. The king or queen retains the right to make laws and policy. Most, but not all, of these monarchies are in Africa and the Middle East.

KUWAIT AND OMAN

Kuwait and Oman are small, oil-rich countries on the Persian Gulf. Both have monarchs who rule with absolute authority. Kuwait is ruled by Sheikh Sabah, who is the prime minister as well as the emir, or monarch. Members of his family hold most of the important posts in government. There is a parliament, but Sheikh Sabah has the final word on all its decisions. This has led to conflict in recent years. Oman is ruled by Sultan Qaboos. He, too, is prime minister in his country. His policies are popular, because he has used money from sales of oil to improve the country's basic services, such as roads, transportation, and power supplies.

Kuwait is a very wealthy country, because it has huge supplies of oil. The money from oil sales has been invested in the economy.

LIECHTENSTEIN

Liechtenstein is a very small, wealthy country in Europe. It lies between Switzerland and Austria. Liechtenstein is a principality, which means it is a monarchy that has a prince as its head of state. At a time when most nations have reduced their monarch's power, Liechtenstein has instead recently increased it. In 2004, a new constitution gave the prince even more authority. Hans-Adam II can now veto, or stop, any law proposed by parliament. He appoints, and can dismiss, the prime minister and all ministers. The prince remains extremely popular with the people, and a referendum on removing his power to veto any law was overwhelmingly defeated in 2012.

UNDERSTANDING BETTER

THE ARAB SPRING

In 2011, in North Africa and the Middle East, a series of popular protests against the undemocratic governments of several countries in the region began. The protests are now known as "The Arab Spring." During these protests, thousands of people in Morocco called for reform. To stop the protests, the Moroccan king offered a new constitution, which won approval in a referendum. However, opponents of the king state that no real changes have actually been made. They say that the king can still veto most of the government's decisions. The king's cautious modernizing looks likely to continue.

In Liechtenstein, Prince Hans-Adam is head of state, but in 2004 he handed over the day-to-day running of the principality to his son, Crown Prince Alois.

The Arab World

Some of the monarchies of the Middle East are newer than those in Europe, and almost all of their kings have more absolute power. The monarchs of the Middle East often claim their authority from Islam, saying that God has given them the right to rule.

SAUDI ARABIA

The kingdom of Saudi Arabia was founded in 1932. Saudi Arabia is the birthplace of Islam, and the monarchy there describes itself as Islamic. Saudi Arabia is an absolute monarchy, although the king must follow Islamic law and the Islamic holy book, the Quran. No national elections have ever been held in Saudi Arabia, and no political parties are allowed. The king is also the country's prime minister, and makes all of its laws. Members of the royal family have leading positions in government, although religious leaders also play a part. Saudi Arabia is a very rich country, because it has huge supplies of oil.

The present king of Saudi Arabia is King Abdullah. He has made some small political reforms in his country, such as giving women the right to vote.

JORDAN

Between Saudi Arabia in the east, and Israel in the west, lies Jordan. The country became a kingdom in 1946. The Hashemites is the country's ruling family. King Abdullah II appoints the government, approves legislation, and can dismiss parliament. Since 2011, however, he has taken some steps toward some democratic reforms.

When King Hussein of Jordan (on the left) died in 1999, his son Abdullah (on the right) became king. King Abdullah appointed a new prime minister in 2013, to introduce political and economic reforms. They are beginning to bring more democracy to the country.

UNDERSTANDING BETTER

WEALTH AND POWER

In the small, oil-rich states of Bahrain and Qatar, the powerful ruling monarchs have also begun to introduce some political reforms. The United Arab Emirates is a federation of seven small states, which is governed by a Supreme Council made up of their seven emirs, or monarchs. The emirs are all absolute rulers. They have used the money made by selling their countries' oil to create better systems within their countries, such as improved health, education, and transportation systems. Do you think this may have affected the level of opposition to the emirs' undemocratic rule?

Monarchy in Africa

There are three monarchies in Africa. These are in Morocco, in North Africa, and Lesotho and Swaziland in South Africa. The first two are constitutional monarchies. However, in Swaziland, the king rules with absolute authority.

HEREDITARY MONARCHY

Morocco is a country on the Atlantic coast of northwest Africa. The monarchs of this country have all claimed to be descendants of the Islamic prophet, Mohammed. The monarchs state that this gives them the right to rule. Although Morocco has a constitution and an elected parliament, the current monarch, King Mohammed VI, holds a great deal of power. His decisions can override those of parliament, and he can dismiss parliament, if he chooses. The king can also issue decrees that have the force of law.

King Mohammed VI of Morocco (on the left) succeeded his father as king in 1999. Since The Arab Spring, he has introduced some reforms to the constitution. He says that he intends to fight against the high levels of poverty in his country, and give more rights to women.

LESOTHO

The country of Lesotho is surrounded entirely by another nation, South Africa. The prime minister of Lesotho is the head of government, but the king is the country's head of state. The king of Lesotho, Letsie III, has no real political authority, and his role is mainly ceremonial. Lesotho is an extremely poor country, and some people think it would benefit if the monarchy there was removed and the country became part of South Africa, which is a wealthier nation.

UNDERSTANDING BETTER

SWAZILAND

Swaziland has the last absolute monarchy in Africa. The country has a parliament, and elections to vote people into it are held every five years. Despite this, parliament can only advise the king about policies. King Mswati III rules by decree, and claims that the country is not ready for multiparty politics. He stamps out opposition, controls the media, and spends public money on his luxurious lifestyle. Most people in Swaziland live in extreme poverty and hunger. Life expectancy for men is just 50 years. Some people are fighting for democracy in their country. What effect do you think the country's poverty might have on the ability of protesters to bring about political change?

King Mswati III is known as "the lion," and has many wives.

Monarchy in Asia

Two of the oldest and most powerful monarchies in the world once existed in Asia—in China and in Japan. China became a republic in 1911 but Japan still has an emperor to this day. Other monarchies in southeast Asia are also ancient kingdoms, but the power of the royal rulers varies greatly from kingdom to kingdom.

SMALL KINGDOMS

Malaysia is a federation of nine small kingdoms, and has an unusual system of monarchy. Every five years, the sultans of each state elect a monarch from among themselves. He is called the paramount leader. The monarch is Malaysia's head of state, but the Malaysian government holds the country's real political power.

In Brunei, on the other hand, the sultan's rule is absolute. Since 1962, the Sultan of Brunei has governed by decree, and no elections are held in the country. Brunei is an extremely oil-rich country, and the sultan is one of the world's wealthiest men.

This Thai man is holding a portrait of King Bhumibol Adulyadej, after attending the celebrations for the king's 85th birthday, in 2012.

REVERENCE AND RESPECT

Thailand has had a monarchy since 1238. Today, the country is a constitutional monarchy, so the king of Thailand has no political power. However, unlike in many countries, the monarchy of Thailand commands great reverence and respect from its people. It is even against Thai law to criticize the king, and the state strongly enforces this law. The present king of Thailand, Bhumibol Adulyadej, took the throne in June 1946, and is currently the world's longest-reigning monarch.

King Jigme Khesar Namgyel Wangchuck is the monarch in Bhutan. Since he came to the throne in 2006, he has promised to continue his father's work in bringing more democracy to his country.

UNDERSTANDING BETTER

WILLINGNESS TO CHANGE

Nepal and Bhutan are both small, poor countries in the Himalayas, but have very different histories. In 2008, Nepal abolished its monarchy, after a long and violent campaign. The country is now a republic. Bhutan, by contrast, has a new and forward-looking king. The king has reduced royal powers, and introduced constitutional monarchy to Bhutan. Do you think this willingness to change has made it more likely that the monarchy will survive in Bhutan?

Dynasties

One of the arguments given in favor of monarchy is that the continuity of leadership within one family brings stability to a country. If a family rules well, the people of a country will continue to support them. Support for one ruling family, or dynasty, is often seen in republics, as well as in monarchies.

DYNASTY IN INDIA

Following its independence from Britain in 1945, India has been governed by three generations of one family, the Nehru–Gandhis. Jawaharlal Nehru campaigned for independence, then served as Indian prime minister, until 1964. His daughter, Indira Gandhi, had long terms as prime minister (1966–1977, 1980–1984), until she was assassinated in 1984. Her son, Rajiv, succeeded her for five years. He, too, was assassinated. The power of the Nehru-Gandhi dynasty even reached to Rajiv's widow, Sonia. She led the family's political party, Congress, to election victory in 2004. However, Sonia refused to become prime minister.

This is a statue of Indira Gandhi, the daughter of India's first prime minister after independence. As prime minister herself, she commanded great respect in India. The Gandhi dynasty held office in India for many years.

UNDERSTANDING BETTER

KEEP IT IN THE FAMILY

The Bush family has also been prominent in US political life. George H.W. Bush, and his son, George W. Bush, have both been president, and George W's brother, Jeb Bush, has also been in the political spotlight. Wives have often followed their husbands into high office, too. Imelda Marcos is the widow of former president of the Philippines, Ferdinand Marcos. Like her husband, Imelda Marcos also had a long political career, and has been voted into many positions in the Philippine government. Why do you think electors make the choice to vote for members of the same family? Do they feel safest with "what they know?"

THE KENNEDYS

The United States has seen loyalty to political family dynasties, too. From the 1960s, the Kennedys were often described as the United States' "royal family." The sons and grandsons of Joseph "Joe" Kennedy held political office for the Democrat party. The most famous of them was John F. Kennedy, thirty-fifth president of the United States, who was assassinated in 1963. The Kennedy dynasty has been struck by tragedy over the years, with Joe Kennedy's wife, Rose, outliving four of her children, and three of her grandchildren.

John F. Kennedy served as US president from 1961 to 1963. After his death, his brothers "Bobby" and "Ted" Kennedy both served as senators. Bobby Kennedy was assassinated in 1968, during his campaign to become president.

CHAPTER FOUR

The Future for Monarchy

Many monarchies have disappeared during the last century. This has led some people to question whether monarchy, in its present form, can still have any part to play in modern, democratic societies. If monarchy is to survive, it will need to reform itself and adapt to change, today and in the future.

A UNIFYING SYMBOL

Monarchists argue that constitutional monarchs play an important unifying role in their countries. Monarchs have no link with political opinion, and their view is impartial, so that people of all political opinions can feel loyalty to them. A monarch's concern is for the good of the whole country. Monarchs are also a powerful symbol of a nation, and a link with the past. In their role as a head of state, monarchs can represent the nation to the rest of the world. There is no threat of absolute rule, because real political power still lies with democratically elected representatives.

In the United Kingdom, the Queen's grandson, Prince William, is a very popular figure. He is set to inherit the throne after his father, Prince Charles.

PRACTICAL BENEFITS

Having a separate head of state also frees a country's prime minister to govern. Not all politicians are good at ceremonial duties, and a monarch has been brought up from birth to understand his or her ceremonial role. The monarch can host foreign visitors, travel the world in the nation's interest, and carry out all the ceremonial duties required of a head of state.

OUT OF DATE

Critics of monarchy say it represents an out-of-date view of the world. They argue that success in society should depend on a person's abilities and hard work, not on an accident of birth. Critics of monarchy say it encourages inequality, and is also linked to a single state religion, in a time when society includes people of many faiths, and those with none.

Crowds fill the streets to celebrate Queen's Day in the Netherlands. A monarch can inspire a sense of loyalty in people, which brings them closer together.

UNDERSTANDING BETTER

THE SURVIVAL OF MONARCHY

Prince Charles, heir to the British throne, has said: "Something as curious as the monarchy won't survive unless you take account of people's attitudes. After all, if people don't want it, they won't have it." What do you think Prince Charles means by this?

Monarchy in Australia

Queen Elizabeth II of the United Kingdom is also Queen of Australia. She is represented in Australia by a governor-general, who is Australian by birth, and by governors in each state. In this former part of the British Empire, and member of the Commonwealth, the move toward becoming a republic has gained considerable support.

AGAINST MONARCHY

Republicans in Australia argue that their head of state should not be someone living on the other side of the world. They also object, in principle, to monarchy, because the power of kings and queens is achieved only by the accident of birth, rather than through hard work, or talent.

The Australian parliament meets in the country's capital, Canberra. It consists of two houses, the House of Representatives, and the senate. The government of Australia is completely separate from the United Kingdom.

A REFERENDUM

In 1999, Australia held a referendum about whether or not to become a republic. To many people's surprise, the result was not in favor of change. This may have been because voters did not like the proposal, within the referendum, that the new head of state should be chosen by parliament. They favored a directly-elected president instead, which is the type of presidency seen in the United States. A poll, taken in October 2011, found that support for constitutional change in Australia is at its lowest level for 20 years. It seems there will be no more public debate on the subject, at least until the end of the reign of Queen Elizabeth II.

UNDERSTANDING BETTER

A DIVERSE POPULATION

In the past, a significant part of Australia's population was British in origin. In the nineteenth and twentieth centuries, many British people chose to emigrate to Australia. Today, Australia is home to people who have moved there from a variety of countries other than Britain. Many immigrants have arrived from southern Europe and from Asian countries, so Australian society is now much more multicultural than it once was. This diversity may have strengthened republican feeling at the end of the twentieth century. Today, however, that feeling seems to be waning.

In a referendum in 2011, the people of Australia decided to keep the monarchy.

A New Role

Monarchs and members of royal families today have very different roles than in the past. Most monarchs are now investing time and thought in modernizing their image, while continuing to fulfill their nonpolitical functions.

A NEW IMAGE

Monarchs are certainly no longer the remote figures they once were. Today, monarchs have greater contact with the people, cultivate a more "ordinary" image, and are constantly in the media. This is especially true of the younger generation of royals, who have become part of our modern-day "celebrity culture." The attention that royalty commands is now also put to good use to help people in need. Charitable work is an important part of the role of many monarchs today. They support charities, and work as ambassadors for good causes—in their own countries, and abroad. Monarchs also attract tourism to their countries—

drawing in people who are fascinated to see a history that they may not have in their own country. The revenue created by tourists visiting countries, such as Britain, to see the monarchy is significant.

Tourism is a very important industry in Britain today. The money that tourists spend when they go to see the sights connected with the monarchy creates jobs and wealth in the country.

ABSOLUTE MONARCHS

The fundamental democratic idea that people should be allowed to have an active part in electing their government has gained widespread acceptance around the world. With this democratic ideal in mind, people in countries with absolute monarchies are pushing for change. It seems likely that the tide of change will be with these campaigners in the years ahead, and their monarchs will have to reform, whether they want to or not.

This mother and child live in Sweden, a country where the standard of living is high. Sweden has had a monarchy for hundreds of years, but, today, the monarch has no political role.

UNDERSTANDING BETTER

MONARCHY AND LIVING STANDARDS

The United Nations Human Development Index ranks countries by income, health, literacy, and civil liberties, to show the overall quality of life for people who live there. The top ten nations include eight monarchies (Canada, Norway, Australia, Sweden, Belgium, Netherlands, Japan, United Kingdom) and two republics (United States, Iceland). Do you think the fact that these countries are monarchies is relevant to the quality of life for people who live there?

What Have You Learned?

Monarchy is the oldest form of government in history. Until one hundred years ago, it was also still the most common form of government worldwide. Today, that picture has changed, but many stable monarchies remain in place around the world.

SHARING POWER

In its long history, monarchy has often brought about progress. Strong leaders have invested effort and money in their countries, which encouraged social and economic progress. Over the centuries, kings and queens learned to share power with other institutions of government. Today, constitutional monarchy, in which the monarch has no political power and the country's government is elected by the people, is considered normal.

King Henry VIII of England (1509–1547) ruled at a time when monarchs had a great deal of power. He controlled every aspect of government in his kingdom, but he was wise enough to consult with parliament and other powerful individuals in making policies and raising taxes to pay for them.

INFLUENCE OF MONARCHS

If most monarchs are without political power today, they are not without influence. Monarchs are powerful symbols of unity and continuity, and represent their countries abroad. They also promote good causes. However, they are not without their critics. In Australia, and elsewhere, a significant minority of people would like to see their country become a republic. The debate over the future of monarchy continues, but history has shown how flexible it can be. The institution of monarchy is most likely to survive in the modern world if it remains willing and able to change.

UNDERSTANDING BETTER

IS MONARCHY WORKING?

In a poll in Britain in 2012, 80 percent of the people questioned voted in favor of retaining the monarchy. This was 10 percent more than 20 years previously. Just 13 percent favored a republic. In a poll in Canada, 51 percent supported keeping the Queen as head of state. In contrast, the last two presidents of Germany, whose role is also largely ceremonial, have been forced to resign before completing their terms. Does this suggest that modern monarchy is working? What do you think?

Young royals in Europe, such as Prince Harry in the United Kingdom, bring a more modern image to the monarchy. Prince Harry is unlikely ever to be king, but his behavior may affect how people view the monarchy in the future.

GLOSSARY

abdicated resigned from the throne

abolished removed, or ended

assassinated deliberately killed

Aztecs a civilization that flourished in Mexico in the fourteenth to sixteenth centuries

Buddhism a religion from Asia that follows the teachings of Buddha

ceremony the formal actions carried out on an important occasion

civil war a conflict between two groups in the same country

colony an area of land that is taken over and ruled by another country

constitution a set of rules and principles that explains how a nation should be governed

constitutional monarchy monarchy in which the power of the monarch is limited by a constitution

coronation the ceremony that crowns a monarch

decrees rules made by kings or queens

democractic a system of government where the people take part

deposed forced to leave power

descendants people who are the relatives of people who lived long ago

dictators leaders who rule with absolute power

divine like a god

dynasty a family of rulers or holders of high office

emperor the ruler of an empire

executive branch the branch of government that initiates policy and carries it out

federal a system where several states are ruled by a central government

hereditary monarchy monarchy where the ruler's child, or nearest relative, becomes king or queen after them

imperial the rule of an emperor

Incas a civilization that flourished in Peru in the fifteenth and sixteenth centuries

Islam a religion that follows the guidance of a prophet named Mohammed

judiciary the branch of government consisting of the judges and law courts

legislature the branch of government that debates policy and makes laws

patriotism a love for and loyalty to your country

prophet someone who predicts the future, a holy person

referendum a vote open to all citizens on an issue of national importance

reform political or social change

republic a democracy where the head of state is also elected, rather than a hereditary monarch

revolution a violent upheaval to overthrow a ruler or bring radical change

sovereign the person with supreme authority over a country

Soviet Union a union of countries in eastern Europe, led by Russia, which lasted until 1991

succession coming to the throne after the previous monarch

successors people who come to the throne after the previous monarch

tsars emperors of Russia

Versailles a beautiful palace built in Paris by the French king Louis XIV

veto the power to stop a decision or a law being made

FOR MORE INFORMATION

BOOKS

Ganeri, Anita. *Kings & Queens: The History of the British Monarchy.* Andover, UK: Haynes Publishing, 2011.

Gelletly, LeeAnne. *Monarchy: Major Forms of World Government.* Broomall, PA: Mason Crest Publishers, 2012.

Gombrich, E. H. *A Little History of the World.* New Haven, CT: Yale University Press, 2008.

WEBSITES

Find out more about Britain's monarchy and its history at:
britainexpress.com/History/monarchs.htm

Discover more about kings and queens at:
ducksters.com/history

Find out more about the British monarchy at:
royal.gov.uk

INDEX